Faerie Houses III
Coloring Book

Stephany Elsworth

Copyright © 2021 by Stephany Elsworth
All rights reserved. No part of this publication may be reproduced, distributed, or transmitted in any form or by any means, including photocopying, recording, or other electronic or mechanical methods, without the prior written permission of the author.

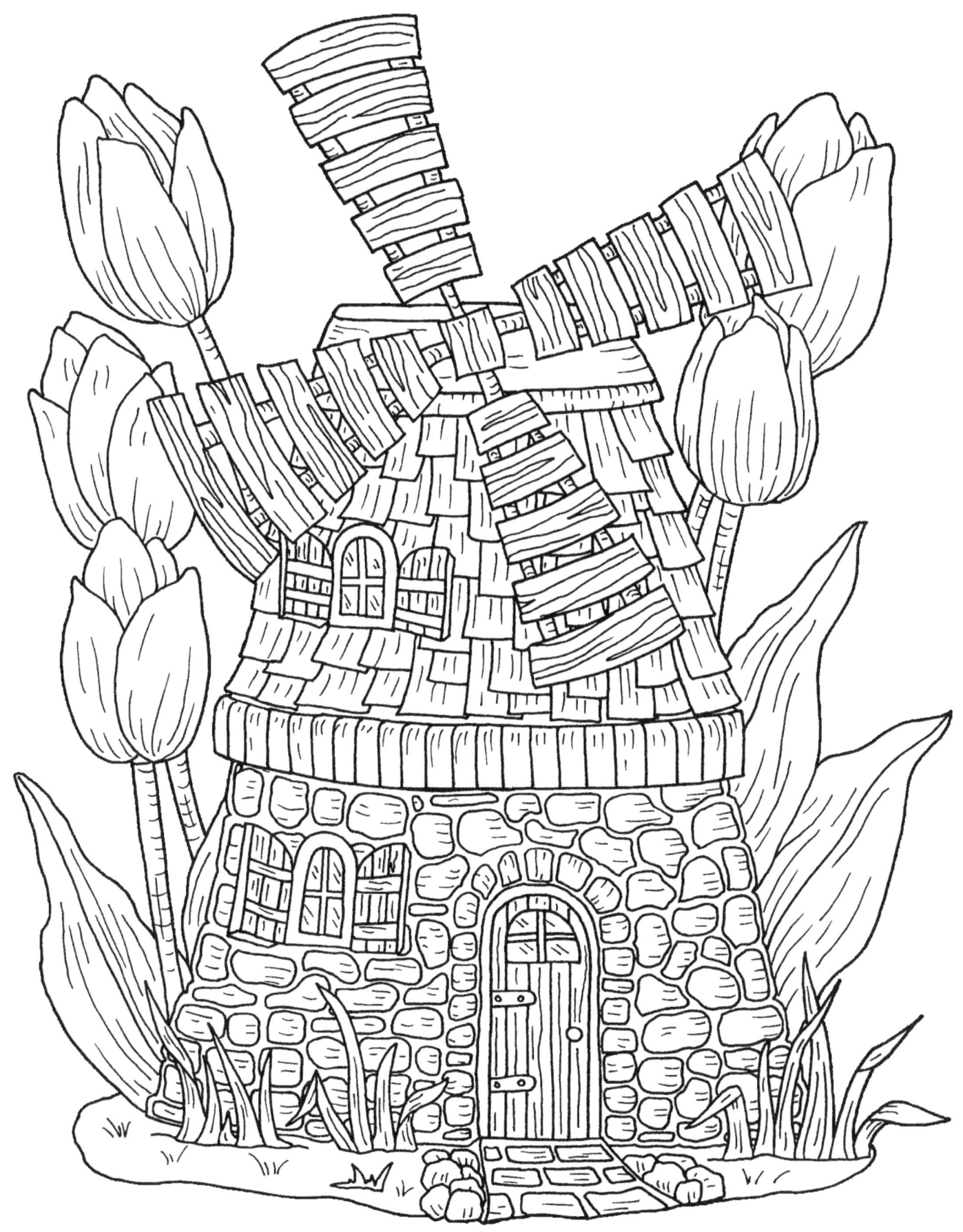

www.ingramcontent.com/pod-product-compliance
Lightning Source LLC
Chambersburg PA
CBHW081700220526
45466CB00009B/2837